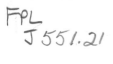

VOLCANOES
INSIDE AND OUT

BY D. M. SOUZA

ILLUSTRATIONS BY
DEBORAH AND ALLAN DREW-BROOK-CORMACK

On My Own

SCIENCE

M Millbrook Press/Minneapolis

Millbrook Press
A division of Lerner Publishing Group
241 First Avenue North
Minneapolis, MN 55401 U.S.A.

Website address: www.lernerbooks.com

Library of Congress Cataloging-in-Publication Data

Souza, D. M. (Dorothy M.)
    Volcanoes inside and out / by D. M. Souza ; illustrations by Deborah Drew-Brook-
Cormack and Allan Drew-Brook-Cormack.
        p.   cm. — (On my own science)
    Includes bibliographical references.
    ISBN: 1–57505–761–1 (lib. bdg. : alk. paper)
    1. Volcanoes—Juvenile literature. 2. Plate tectonics—Juvenile literature. I. Drew-
Brook-Cormack, Deborah, ill. II. Drew-Brook-Cormack, Allan, ill. III. Title. IV. Series.
QE521.3.S64 2006
551.21—dc22   2004027897

Manufactured in the United States of America
1 2 3 4 5 6 – DP – 11 10 09 08 07 06

for M.C.
—DMS

Success to all the future young volcanologists
—Allan & Deborah

The mountain shakes and rumbles.

Hot steam and burning rocks

shoot high into the air.

The sky turns fiery red, yellow,
and orange.
A volcano is waking from its sleep.

People long ago believed volcanoes were
the work of a fire god named Vulcan.
They said that Vulcan had a workshop
deep inside a mountain.
There he made thunderbolts
and weapons for other gods.
The mountain spit out hot rocks
and steam when Vulcan was busy.
Since then, people have learned
that volcanoes are not caused by Vulcan.
They begin deep inside Earth.

Inside Earth

Far beneath our planet's land and oceans
is a thick layer of rock.
This rocky layer is called Earth's crust.
It is many miles thick.
The crust is not whole like a pie crust.
It is broken into large parts called plates.
The plates fit together like pieces
of a giant jigsaw puzzle.

The layer of Earth below the plates
is also rocky and very hot.
The fiery heat melts rocks
into a thick liquid called magma.
The magma bubbles and churns
beneath the plates.
The churning magma makes the plates
move a few inches each year.

Sometimes, plates bump into one another.

The ground shakes and rumbles.

We call it an earthquake.

Other times, plates move apart.

Then hot magma shoots through

an opening called a vent.

We say a volcano is erupting.

Most volcanoes erupt along the edges

of Earth's plates.

But once in a while,

they erupt in the middle of plates.

Some volcanoes begin on land.

Others begin under the ocean.

They grow slowly.

Most of them cannot be seen.

But some underwater volcanoes grow to be giants.

They rise up out of the water.

These giant volcanoes form islands such as the Hawaiian Islands.

What makes magma move upward?

Gases form in the fiery heat inside Earth.

These gases move upward.

They mix with magma and make it rise.

Sometimes the gases make magma
flow slowly from a vent.

Other times, gases make magma
suddenly erupt out of Earth.

Gases in a bottle of soda
do the same thing.

Turn a bottle upside down.

Gas bubbles slowly rise.

Shake the bottle.

Then open it carefully.

The soda gases burst out of the opening.

Once magma escapes from Earth,
it is called lava.
Hot lava burns everything in its path.
It can destroy homes, cars,
and entire towns or cities.
Steam, rocks, and ash
also burst out of the volcano.
The rocks can be as small as baseballs
or bigger than basketballs.

After a volcano erupts,
ash and rock pile up around the vent.
They build until they look like the sides
of a giant empty bowl.
The bowl is called a crater.
The stories you are about to read are
about three different kinds of volcanoes.
Each story is true.

The Sleeping Giant

Mount Saint Helens is a volcano
in the State of Washington.
In 1980, it had been quiet
for more than one hundred years.

Snow covered it in the winter.
Flowers bloomed in the summer.
People could see the mountain's
towering cone shape in the distance.
They thought the mountain looked
like a sleeping giant.

The giant awoke one spring day.
Earthquakes began shaking
the snowy top of Mount Saint Helens.
Magma rose inside the mountain.
It made one side of the mountain swell.
Then a powerful earthquake
shook the ground around the mountain.

Hot lava, gases, and ash burst
out of the swollen side.
The mountain soon blew its top.
Flowing lava quickly melted the snow.
The water mixed with rocks and soil.
This mudflow moved down the volcano
faster than a speeding car on a freeway.

The volcano's mudflow swept away trees,
trucks, cabins, and animals.
In some places, the mudflow was taller
than a building with six floors.
Ash and steam rose above the explosion.
They formed a cloud that hid the Sun.
Winds carried the cloud miles away.
One city became so dark
that lights had to be turned on all day.
Some people wore face masks
when they went outside.
They were afraid of choking
on the dust and ash.
At least 57 people lost their lives in the
volcano's eruption.
Many birds and other animals died too.